CONTENTS

Chapter 1: The Beginning.   3

Chapter 3: Losing everything.   14

Chapter 4: The long road back.   18

Chapter 5: World class training.   22

Chapter 6: Tough Decisions.   27

Chapter 7: Welcome to the real world.   32

Chapter 8: Disaster.   35

Chapter 9: A living nightmare.   38

Chapter 10: Moving forward.   41

Chapter 11: New challenges.   45

Chapter 12: A different life.   50

CHAPTER 1: THE BEGINNING.

I remember it as if it were yesterday, I was five years old, every Saturday morning I would don my leotard, and attend the gymnastics club with my best friend at the local leisure centre. However, today wasn't like every other Saturday. After weeks of pleading, mum had agreed I could go trampolining, but only after I had finished my gymnastics class. I remember gazing across the big sports hall, beyond the gymnastics equipment, to the corner of the hall sectioned off by large green curtains hanging from the ceiling. The curtains were netted from halfway up, allowing you only a glimpse of what was happening behind them. All I could see were people appearing, and rising up, before disappearing back behind the immense green shield. I remember staring up at the large clock, watching the hands, willing them to move faster, and trying to work out how long I had until I could join in the fun.

I was already trampolining once a week on a leisure centre course, there was something magical about jumping up and down on a webbed piece of material, held to a steel frame by 118 metal springs. It captured my heart immediately. I was desperate to join my sister and start learning at the 'proper', competitive trampoline club. When my gym session finally finished, I wandered over to the curtain. Although I had been looking forward to this moment I'm a naturally shy person and found myself full of nerves. I built up some courage and ventured behind the curtain. I quickly found my big sister and she introduced me to the coach. He was a lovely man, who would become like a grandad to me, he could tell I was nervous but convinced me to "have a go". I climbed up the large steel legs using the support chains as a step, across the thick blue matted frame and onto the trampoline bed. I slowly walked across the soft, bouncy bed to the large red centre cross.

I paused...looked at my sister, the coach said again, "have a go". I bent my legs, pushed down and jumped.

Before long, I had given up gymnastics so I could spend more time trampolining and soon I started doing competitions, my first a small club competition. I remember the mixed feelings of nervousness and excitement as I stood on the trampoline waiting to compete. I turned to the judges, raised my arms, indicating the start of my competition, then began my well practiced routine. Ten moves later I had successfully completed my routine, I was so excited. I finished my last move and immediately turned to find my parents in the crowd, I waved and walked off the trampoline towards them, so proud of myself. I finished second. If I had stood still, instead of looking for my parents I would have won! Points are deducted if you do not stop and stand still when you finish. I soon learned, never making that mistake again!

The size and level of the my competitions gradually grew bigger, from club to county, county to regional, regional to national. My trampoline coaches, John and Nigel, believed I had talent and I was soon training five times a week with the elite
squad, three times next door, and twice up in London. I quickly got into a routine of racing in from school, doing my homework, before getting ready to go training. My parents took on the role of personal chauffeur, driving me to London, and
around the country to various competitions at weekends. My trampoline club became my second home and my training partners, their parents and our coaches, became one big family.

After a long season training and competing, I finally achieved my goal, qualifying for the British National Championships. The first weekend in July 1994 would be, to me, the most important weekend of my life so far, competing in the biggest
competition of my trampoline career. On the Friday evening before the competition began, the competitors were allowed to attend a training session in the competition venue. I gathered to-

gether my training gear and with mum, made the short journey to Gillingham where the competition was being held. As it was the National finals, it could have been held anywhere in the country, but that year the Black Lion Leisure Centre at Gillingham had the task of hosting this event. As I walked into
the hall I felt my heart start to race, my hands becoming sweaty as I took in the image in front of me. The hall was set up like a normal competition but everything seemed more professional, more polished than any competition I had been to
before. Great Britain (GB) flags were hanging on the wall and there were lots of people rushing around making the finishing touches, ensuring everything was in place for the following morning. I found my team mates and coach and cautiously
made my way over to the trampolines where my group were warming up.

It was now the competition day, and my warm ups and set routine had gone as planned. I just had my voluntary routine to go. I heard the marshall calling my name and quickly made myself known, I was next to compete. I was wearing my
new, green 'lucky' leotard, my family were watching anxiously in the crowd, everything was ready, all I had to do was get through my second, harder routine. As I turned to present to the judges, I smiled, I might be feeling nervous I thought to
myself, but I'm not going to let the judges know that. My team mates were standing attentively by the side of the trampoline, spotting, ready to push me back on if I got too near the edge. Nigel was holding the crash mat, ready to push it in
should anything go wrong. It was more of a security blanket than a necessity. I gave Nigel one last glance, he gave me a reassuring nod, I started my jumps.

As I finished my last jump and stood on the trampoline bed, the first person I looked at, as always, was Nigel. If I received a smile from him I knew I had done well. He placed the mat on the floor and looked up, his serious looking face gradually breaking into a

5

big grin. I ran to find my parents in the crowd, they greeted me with smiles and hugs of congratulations. Everyone was pleased. I finished 11th overall, missing the final, by the smallest of possible margins 0.1

point. I felt a mix of emotions, I was frustrated I had come so close to my dream, but I had also jumped better than ever before, receiving a personal best score. As it was the British National finals, at the end of the competition, all competitors were asked to gather outside of the sports hall, ready to be marched in to the crowd. Over 200 trampolinists gathered in the allocated area, I stood there waiting patiently in my leotard taking it all in. Looking around I easily spotted the performers who, like myself, were experiencing their first ever nationals, waiting in anticipation, wondering what to expect. At the same time I could also identify the well experienced trampolinists who had obviously been through this routine numerous times before.

We were ushered to the entrance of the hall, the officials instructing us to keep the noise down. Everything went quiet, a sense of calm filled the area. Suddenly we heard the start of the music and it was all stations go as a line of over 200

competitors made their way out of the hall to a crowd clapping in time to Tina Turner, 'You're simply the best'. The atmosphere was electric and I was in awe as I walked out alongside faces I recognised as being the best in the British trampoline

team and the World. Individuals I aspired to be like. When everyone was in the hall, we were asked to stand for our national anthem. As I turned to look at the British flag I had an immense feeling of pride and satisfaction, it was a feeling I

relished and definitely one I wanted to have again. As the first day of competition came to an end. For me it was also the end of my nationals, for the lucky finalists they still had the most important day of competition to come and part of me wished

I would be joining them. I had just had the best experience of my life so far and loved every single minute of the competition. It was like an addiction, and I had definitely caught the bug and wanted more.

CHAPTER 2: GREAT BRITAIN SELECTION.

I remember grabbing my things and rushing out of school as soon as I heard the end of day bell ring. We weren't allowed to take our coats to our last lessons, so I had
to fold mine tightly into a ball so it would fit discreetly into a carrier bag enabling me to take it to my lesson. If I didn't, it would mean walking back to my form
room, before I could start the trek out of school and up the hill to the bus stop. I had decided returning to my form room would add unnecessary time onto my journey home, and during April 1996, that was precious time I couldn't afford to
waste. I was thirteen and the only thing on my mind was to get home, as I was desperate to see what the postman had left on our door mat. I was waiting for what seemed like a lifetime for a letter to arrive. I can't describe how much I longed for the postman to deliver the letter that could bring with it life changing news. The only time I had felt like this before was when I was waiting anxiously for my 11 plus results.

I turned the key in the lock, pushed open the front door and quickly scanned the envelopes, looking for my name. There it was, a letter addressed to me. I knew instantly it was what I had been waiting for, the British Trampoline Federation

stamp on the envelope being a big clue! With butterflies in my stomach and my heart racing, I nervously opened the letter. I didn't feel this nervous when I jumped at competitions, but whatever was written in this letter meant more than winning a medal at a national competition. This letter was from the GB National trampoline squad. I read the type,
"Dear Natalie, we are pleased to tell you...",
I stopped, pleased to tell me? That means good news, I thought. My butterflies disappeared and my racing heart was now beating vigorously with excitement. I continued to
read with disbelief, I could see the words on the paper but it took a while to sink in. I had been selected to represent GB at the World Age Group Games (WAGG) in Canada. I had done it! I couldn't believe it, I was actually going to represent my
country in trampolining. It was something I had always dreamed of and for me it had come true.

Everyone was so happy for me especially my parents, but the selection also bought with it an expensive bill we had to find the money to pay. Unfortunately, as trampolining is an amateur sport, competitors selected to jump at the WAGG are
required to pay for the event themselves, which includes flights, hotel, competition entry fee, GB kit and food! With the event being held in Canada it was going to be quite an expensive trip. Luckily my trampoline club quickly rallied around
organising fundraising events to help my parents fund the trip. Trying to raise some money also meant I had the chance to appear in local newspapers, on radio stations and television to appeal to local businesses, hoping for any contribution in the form of sponsorship. With all the attention I felt like a mini celebrity.

The competition was in August, but before that I still had two more national competitions and the British National Finals in July. The hard work was only just beginning. After receiving my selection I was on a high and my confidence grew
and grew. Training went well, and the National finals, held in the

National Exhibition Centre (NEC) in Birmingham, provided an opportunity to see how I was progressing. I can recall the first time I walked into the arena, I had no idea how huge the NEC was and was completely unprepared for what I saw. It took my breath away, never having seen a hall so big. I had definitely never jumped in anywhere even half the size of the NEC arena. It was completely different to any competition I had previously attended. The spectators were not allowed anywhere near to the competition floor and from the seats where my mum and dad would be sitting we just looked like ants running around on the floor. I can't explain how daunting it felt to a thirteen year old girl jumping in somewhere so big!

Amazingly I managed to focus on my routines and actually jumped better than ever. After a long hard weekend and five competition routines later, I finished fourth in my age group, and for the first time had competed in the senior ladies event, where I finished fifteenth. As I had been selected to compete in Canada I was expected by my coach, and the GB coaches, to finish in the top four. With the pressure of competing in a new venue, knowing I should finish high up, as well as the nature of the sport, anything can happen. To hold it together and do so well was a brilliant result, I was over the moon and felt like I definitely deserved my place on the team. The next six weeks flew by, I spent every spare minute training in preparation for the WAGG, as it was school holidays I was able to train during the day. It wasn't long before I found myself kitted out in my team tracksuit and sitting on the plane with the rest of the GB team, preparing for the long trip to Canada. The flight went quickly and by the time we had crossed the Atlantic and landed in Vancouver everybody who was part of the trip had got to know each other.

After we arrived, there wasn't much time to relax as we were soon in the competition arena training, being reminded of the reason we were all in Vancouver, to represent our country in trampolin-

ing. We were allocated a couple of days of
training to get used to the venue and the trampolines before it
was the opening ceremony indicating the official start of four
days of competition. There was something incredibly special
about being part of the GB team. I felt like I was someone, as if I
had achieved something that not many people would have the
chance of experiencing. Everyone on the team, which was made
up of at least forty people ranging from nine to twenty years old,
got on well and came together as one
to support each other. I remember walking from our hotel to the
opening ceremony, we were marching in a long line singing together. Our team captain sang the lines,
before we repeated them after him.

> "Everywhere we go, everywhere we go,
> people always ask us, people always ask us,
> who we are, who we are,
> where we come from, where we come from,
> so we tell them, so we tell them,
> we're from Britain, we're from Britain,
> mighty mighty Britain, mighty, mighty Britain,
> and if they can't hear us, and if they can't hear us,
> we shout a little louder, we shout a little louder"

And so it goes on! As we approached the venue the other teams
were outside, when they heard us everyone stopped what they
were doing, and watched as we marched past them, and into the
arena. We were a team operating as one, everyone with the
same goal, everyone meant business. We were the GB team and we
had a reputation to maintain.

As we waited to be marched on for the opening ceremony, there
was a sea of colour constructed by the tracksuits of my fellow competitors, each displaying the colours of their respective
country. The rainbow of colour demonstrated how many different countries were in attendance. Gradually the huge line of

teams in front of us got shorter as each country entered in turn, through the doors into the bright lights and cheers of the spectators. Then it was our turn, my body filled with excitement as I eagerly walked closer to the doors, the deep Canadian voice of the announcer roared, "Great Britain", it was our cue to enter. As I scanned the seats looking for familiar faces, particularly my parents, I saw the red, white and blue of the GB flag being waved ferociously in the crowd. People were waving and cheering, the support for our team was incredible, families and coaches having travelled miles to support their loved ones. As I walked around the arena waving to the spectators I felt a rush of emotions. I felt fantastic, proud, excited, privileged, like I belonged here, and I couldn't wait to compete.

The day soon arrived for my chance to compete. My routines had been going well in training, I was going to compete my hardest routine yet, one that I had never competed before. I remember the morning of my competition walking into the
arena and joining the line of girls who were patiently queueing next to the trampolines. I stood there quietly, waiting for my turn. My body giving me the familiar signs that my anxiety was rising, my legs feeling like jelly, my heart pounding in my chest, my palms becoming sweaty. After the warm up finished my group lined up and we were marched in to be presented to the judges and spectators. One by one we were introduced, our name and country being announced to everyone. It was good hearing;
"From Great Britain, Natalie O'Connor".
I stepped forward and raised my arms, hearing the applause from the crowd, before stepping back into line, getting ready to compete. I completed my usual pre-competition rituals, doing my hair, gluing my leotard, visualising my routine, and chalking my hands, before climbing up on to the trampoline and waiting for the instruction to begin. I turned and presented to the judges, smiling, thinking to myself, "This is it,
this is my chance to show people what I can do. This is what I have been working for". My legs felt weak and wobbly like jelly, but it

was now or never. I took a deep breath, pushed down hard on the red cross and started my jumps. A sense of
relief washed over me as I safely landed my 10th and final skill, feeling the webbed texture of the trampoline bed securely under my feet. I stopped jumping and paused for a moment, taking in the cheers from the crowd, the smiles on my coaches face and the overwhelming feeling of delight that filled my body. I dismounted the trampoline, and hugged my team mates and coaches, the hard work was done, now I
just had to wait.

As the last performer in my age group finished her routine, I left my seat where I had been watching with my parents, and eagerly made my way down to the corridor where the results were pinned up on the wall. Starting from the second page of results, I quickly scanned the names on the printed sheet. I couldn't find my name, my eyes were moving lower and lower down the list, my heart and hopes began to fade, "I thought I had jumped well" I said to myself. Then the list came to an end,
"that's strange?", I thought. I looked back up, this time starting from the very beginning, and there it was, I couldn't believe it, my name was on the very first page of results. I had been in such a rush to find out my position that I had skipped
looking at the top ten places. It didn't cross my mind I would be one of the top ten! I had finished in ninth place, missing the final by one position! Unfortunately in international events the final is the top eight performers, which meant I wouldn't be jumping for GB again at that competition, so I sat back and enjoyed watching the finals, pleased with what I had achieved, before celebrating at the closing ceremony.

I returned home from Canada a very happy person. I had thoroughly enjoyed the experience and had learned a lot. After achieving my goal of representing my country, I realised what I was capable of, the bar had been raised, and I now had a new set of goals and aspirations to aim for. I was on a high and eager to get back into training to prepare for the following season. I had gone to Canada as a girl who was really good at trampolining and showed some potential, I had no expectations. I returned as a GB international trampolinist, ranked top ten in the world for my age group. Now that was something to be proud of.

CHAPTER 3: LOSING EVERYTHING.

"Jump higher, push the trampoline down, work, that's it, now do your barani", my coach Nigel shouted to me.

"Now?", I thought, "this high? blimey".

A barani was, a single, forward somersault with a half twist, a move well within my capabilities, but I was a very powerful trampolinist. I was physically strong and could jump extremely high compared to others my age, it was what I had become known for. So jumping my full height (about 20 foot), then being asked to do a simple move, requiring little power, naturally made me slightly anxious. I could easily over rotate if I didn't get the take off just right. However I wasn't the type of person to argue with, or question my coach he had my full trust, so I did as I was asked. I jumped as high as I could, and took off for a barani. As I came down preparing to land on my back, I wondered what had gone wrong. A barani lands on your feet. I had taken off with every intention of performing a barani but had not twisted when I should have, doing instead an extra three quarter somersault, meaning I had actually

completed a one and three quarter forward somersault, a move I could also do easily, but a move I had never executed by mistake before.

Unfortunately, unbeknown to me at the time, this was the start of what is known as Lost Move Syndrome (LMS), and things were going to get a whole lot worse before they would start getting even slightly better. In trampolining LMS is a mystery, no one knows why some people experience it and others don't. During the time I was going through it, there wasn't a lot of guidance for

performers or coaches about
how best to help people through this awful time. People experience LMS to varying degrees, for some it may be that only one move is affected, whereas others get to the stage where they can not even jump on a trampoline without involuntarily
doing a move, normally a backward somersault. Initially for me, only my barani's were affected. Missing the exit and twist of the skill, and rotating an extra three quarter somersault, became a regular occurrence and it wasn't long before I had
problems with all my forward rotating skills. After feeling that I was finally achieving what I had always wanted, being part of the GB team and getting some recognition for my hard work, it was all taken away from me. I lost all my confidence and belief in myself. Belief that had taken a long time to build up,
belief that I had finally gained after my good result in Canada, belief that was now shattered.

I had been really looking forward to the new season, I had moved up an age group but was confident I would still do well and had plans to maintain my place on the British team. However, 1997 turned out to be a nightmare. My coach didn't know
how to help me. Looking back it must have been as difficult for him as it was for me, seeing his top performer reduced to barely being able to jump. We ended up clashing, arguing and disagreeing about my training. At numerous sessions I would
end up in tears, desperately trying to understand why I was experiencing these move problems, when everything had been going so well, physically nothing had changed. It was an extremely challenging time, I felt lost and alone, like no one
could help me. Despite the difficulties I was having, I still never missed a training session or a competition. I couldn't. Trampolining was who I was, I had dedicated so much of my time, my life, to it, whether I was at the top of my game, or struggling to get by, it was what I knew, it was where my friends were and it was still what I wanted. I was determined to get my moves back from wherever they were hiding. I still had the same dreams and aspir-

ations as before, now I just had a lot more work to do to achieve them.

About halfway through the season, after competing at a couple of competitions I was still struggling and had not gained the qualifying score for the National finals. I was embarrassed and ashamed. I felt like I was letting my coaches, my parents and myself down and I didn't even know why I was having these troubles. Competing also made me confront the issues, it made it all real. Although I was having problems in training, no one except those involved within our small club
network knew. It was almost as if I could pretend to people outside the club and maybe to myself, that it wasn't happening. By trying to compete, I was putting myself out there in front of everyone involved in national trampolining, there was
no where to hide.

Eventually the time came when I decided to leave my much loved club. It was not an easy decision and I had spent a long time thinking about whether it was the right thing to do, it was really only Nigel I wanted to leave. We weren't getting on and although he was responsible for getting me to Canada, I had lost respect and trust in him after the constant disagreements and arguments we were having. I was already intending to change clubs at the end of the season, as Nigel was moving away, so it just meant leaving a few months earlier than planned. The day came when I had to tell John I was going, I remember it so clearly. It was one of the hardest things I have ever had to do. After ten years with the club, John really was like a member of my family. He was such a nice person with a heart of gold, and it broke my heart, and his, telling him I was leaving. Although he didn't want me to leave, John fully
understood and supported my reasons. Things had broken down so much between Nigel and I, I never actually told him I was leaving. So after saying my goodbyes, I walked towards the exit, opened the heavy green door, and turned for one last long
look at the place I had called my second home. Holding back

the tears, I managed half a smile at John before turning back and leaving. The door clicked shut behind me, "An end of an era", I thought. That chapter of my life was well and truly over.

CHAPTER 4: THE LONG ROAD BACK.

Since joining my new club in April 1997 I managed to qualify for the National finals, which quickly came around. As they approached, despite still fighting LMS, I was determined to compete, and managed to struggle through two routines,

finishing in last place. However, the process of rebuilding my skills had already been started by my new coaches, they took me back to basics and completely retaught me all of my moves. Luckily their training facilities were the best in the

country, a purpose built trampoline centre. This meant I had access to a foam pit and could safely regain my confidence and the ability to execute my skills, reassured I could not hurt myself if I did make a mistake.

I landed in the soft spongy foam, the familiar sweaty, musty smell hit me, the dust, unsettled upon my entrance into the pit, rose up into my eyes, but a big grin crept across my face. The last year had been a long, gruelling slog as I tried everything to regain the moves I had 'lost' so quickly. In the space of eighteen months, I had gone from being perfectly happy in my club, ranked ninth in the World, to only just being able to bounce on a trampoline, at a new club, with people I didn't know. As I lay in the pit getting my breath back before starting the huge climb out of the foam, I was excited, confident and proud, feelings I had not felt for a long time. I had just executed a rudi out, the final skill to get back, the last piece I needed to

complete the jigsaw. I was now able to successfully complete all the moves I could do previously. Slowly but surely my confidence grew, as well as regaining my old skills, I even learned new, more

difficult moves. I started the season in March 1998
with the most difficult routine I had ever competed. It felt good,
the old me was back, LMS was in my past. However it had left
me with some insecurities, imprinting its mark on my self-belief,
and it would prove to be something I would never fully be free
from.

Over the next few years I returned to my previous form, achieving good results at the National championships. September 1999
saw my return to the GB team, being selected to compete at the
WAGG in Sun City, South Africa. My return to form physically,
also saw a return to my former self, mentally and emotionally.
Once again, I was 'Natalie, the international trampolinist', I was
achieving my dreams, which gave me the sense of self worth I had
been lacking when I could not perform to my best. Rather than
being ashamed and embarrassed that I could not complete certain skills on the trampoline, I was happy of who I was, eager to
tell people what I could do. After my good performances that year
I was invited to become a regular member of the GB senior squad.
This was a major boost to my confidence and was a great feeling to
have some recognition. The squad consisted of about thirty men
and ladies. Although being on the squad did not guarantee you a
place on the GB team, it was a huge achievement to be recognised
as upcoming talent and a potential future member of this prestigious team.

Time passed and I reached a point in my life where I had to leave
home and go to university. As well as achieving in my sport, I
was getting good grades at school, passing all my exams. Deciding
which university to go to involved considering some important
questions. What trampoline club was near by? How good was the
club? How easily could I get there? The usual factors, such as the
reputation of the university, the local nightlife, the cost of living,
were irrelevant to me. If going to university meant I had to jeop-
ardise my trampolining career, the choice was simple, I wouldn't
go. Luckily, near to a good university for the course I wanted to

do, Sport Science, was the best trampoline club in the country!! The decision was
made.

When the time arrived for me to make the big step of moving out of home and going to university, it was really hard. I am an incredibly shy person and when my parents said goodbye, leaving me in my halls of residence, in a situation where I
didn't know anybody, I was really uncomfortable and felt so alone. The first month at university was awful. I spent every minute wishing I could come home, the people in my halls were friendly, but they seemed loud, confident and outgoing,
everything I wasn't. During this time trampolining was the only constant thing in my life. Everything else I had known, living at home, my school friends, the area I lived in, had changed. Going training was the one part of the day where I felt relaxed, comfortable and normal. When I was on the trampoline I felt free from my worries, it was my chance to escape.

After listening to my parents, who told me every night to, "give it one more day", I eventually settled in and am glad and thankful that I didn't leave. Being at university allowed me to train every day and the coaching I received was the best I
ever had. One of the coaches was a GB squad coach and the people I were training with made up half of the senior GB team. It was a privilege to train there. I remember walking into the sports hall for my first training session. It was empty
except for the two trampolines situated at the far left hand corner. It was a complete contrast to my club at home, which was a purpose built trampoline centre. However, being good is not judged on the quality of your training hall. I looked up
at the people training, immediately recognising all four performers as the elite of GB. I felt my heart race, as it did at competitions, my palms becoming sweaty, my mouth became dry, I was nervous. Although this was only a club training session, I
was about to train with these people. Performers I aspired to be

like. My achievements in trampolining were nothing compared to theirs. So many thoughts raced through my head, "what are they going to think of my training?', "how on earth can I train alongside them?", "I'm going to look rubbish in comparison". I took a deep breath and walked towards the trampolines. The coach, Sandra, who I knew from GB squads and competitions, turned and waved. She was a welcoming lady, with a wealth of knowledge in trampolining and I had the utmost respect for her. After introducing me to her squad, I got stuck in to my training, desperately eager to learn from the best and trying hard to impress everyone there.

CHAPTER 5: WORLD CLASS TRAINING.

My first training session at my new club, soon turned into the first of many and before I knew it was time to go home for the Christmas break. After the first semester passed I had fully settled in to university life, and was thoroughly enjoying my time there. Being at university as an international athlete, compared to being at university as your average student, had some major differences. My student life involved studying, trampolining or going to the gym. I rarely went out drinking.

Alcohol, late nights and training to become a senior international athlete, do not go hand in hand. Making the jump from a youth to a senior international was something I really wanted to achieve, so drinking and late nights were something I was happy to sacrifice.

Training at this club was more intense than any I had previously received. There were less performers to each trampoline and the coaching was one to one. I loved it. During the holidays, rather than miss out on quality training, I chose to make the 140 mile journey, up to my club and back for the two hour training session. It was hard and tiring but worth every minute. Christmas was soon over and it was term time again. In preparation for the approaching season, I upped my training to six times a week, sometimes twice a day. I was keen to compete for my new club, honored to be part of their strong and well respected team. My results that year earned me a place, for the third time, on the WAGG GB team, only narrowly

missing the reserve position for the senior GB team. I was pleased to have been selected but was now aspiring to be part of the senior team, along with my club mates.

I watched the ladies senior team compete at the World Championships that year. Two of the members were my regular training partners, and at the recent National finals I had finished fifth, closely behind the fourth member of the team. So when I was watching, although I wanted to be on the team, I saw myself on a par with them. Rather than looking up to them, in awe, I now identified with the members of the team. They were my friends, my team mates, I already felt part of their team. It was on that trip I started to feel as if I was making it, becoming someone that maybe other people would look up to. I knew if I kept training my dream would come true. I would become a 'proper' trampolinist, competing alongside the very best in the world.

After spending a week in the audience, my time eventually came to compete and I was raring to go. Everything went as planned and I peaked at the right time. After competing my routine, I reached the finals, lying in second place. I was ecstatic. I could not believe it and was so pleased my parents had made the trip out to watch me. The finals start from zero, so any gain you have over your competitors is wiped clean and everyone is given an equal chance to win. The trampolinists in the final also jump in reverse order, meaning the performers in the higher ranked place have to be patient and control their nerves for a bit longer as they wait for the others to compete. This was something I had never experienced before. As I waited for my turn to jump, I visualised my routine perfectly over and over in my head. The sound of the crowd cheering, indicated the end of each competitors performances. I rubbed chalk over my hands and legs, leaving them completely white in preparation for my turn to jump. I didn't have to wait long and the short walk to the trampolines, seemed to last forever. The lights shone down brightly on the arena,
making the white trampoline bed gleam brightly. I finally reached the side of the trampoline, my spotters and coach already in position. I placed my hands on the blue side padding and lifted

myself up, leaving two white chalky hand prints. I
stood on the red cross, rehearsing my routine in my head one last
time, before turning to the five judges sat waiting patiently for me
to begin.

My final performance earned me fifth place. Had I been told before
I jumped, I would finish fifth in the world in my age group, I would
have been over the moon.
However, I had been second before the final, so was left feeling a
little disappointed with my result. Despite this I returned home
with a renewed motivation. Jumping in the final had given me a
taste of how it felt to have the hopes, and support of the British
crowd behind you, as they desperately want you to take a medal
home for GB. It was an incredible feeling having people I had
never met offer me their support and congratulations. I felt important, as if I had a responsibility not only to
myself, my family and my coaches, but also to my country and the
people from GB. On the way home, at the airport people were asking us, the GB team, for autographs. This was something I could
get used to! The next step was the senior
team and I had my sights firmly set on getting the selection I so
desperately wanted.

The following year, 2002, was the European Championships
which was being held in October, in St. Petersburg, Russia. To be
selected I had to be ranked in the top four of the senior ladies at
the end of the season in July. I knew I was capable of a
selection if I performed consistently well. My timetable of lec-
tures in my second year of university had been reduced, which
meant only one thing for me. I could devote more time to training. My hard work and dedication paid off and that season
I performed consistently well. Things were on track for selection
for Russia with one final competition to go, the National finals. As
happened every July, my parents and I made the trip to Birmingham ready for a long weekend of
trampolining. The programme was the same every year, the Sat-

urday involved everybody competing their set and voluntary routines, before those who had jumped well enough competed in the finals on the Sunday. At the end of Saturday, after a long day of competition, I was lying in fourth position, pleased with my performances and excited for the following days final.

When the time arrived for me to compete in the final, I was hoping I had prepared enough to do what was needed. I had been in this position before. My thoughts immediately raced back to Denmark, where my final performance had let me down. I hoped I had learned from that experience, and would execute a stronger performance this time. It was soon my turn to perform. I held it together, securing a strong and consistent performance, my hopes were fulfilled and the marks I received put me into first place. There were only three people left to jump. As the remaining competitors jumped, I watched as the judges raised their scores and the computer screen displaying the results showed their names entering underneath mine. With one competitor left to perform, my name was still at the top of the scoresheet, I was the competitor currently leading the competition, the one to beat. The one performer left to compete was the defending British champion, she didn't disappoint, performing brilliantly and maintaining her title. I was far from disappointed. Although narrowly missing out on becoming British Champion, I had finished in second place. It took time to sink in! At that time, there was only one other person in the country who could trampoline better than me! More importantly, this fabulous result meant I had met the selection criteria for the GB senior team. I had done it. All these years of working hard, the long drives to training, the sacrifices at university, all for this one, important selection were worth it. I had sometimes wondered whether I would ever achieve it, but I refused to give up. I had made a promise to myself all those years before that I was determined to keep, that one day I would be on the senior GB team. I can't explain fully how much it meant. It was special. I had finally made someone of myself, and in a way that made up for the terrible time I had put myself through when I experienced LMS. If I had never reached the GB team then I would never have forgiven myself

for losing my moves. I would have felt I had thrown it all away, the talent and opportunities I were given would have been wasted. Maybe that's why I was so determined to get there. I still felt responsible for losing my moves when things

were going so well, and that had made me feel as if I needed to prove to myself, and others, that I was capable of achieving again, I was stronger than LMS and I would not be beaten by it.

CHAPTER 6: TOUGH DECISIONS.

After gaining my first selection onto the GB senior team, I became a regular team member, attending first the European Championships, where our strong ladies team won the bronze medal, a very proud moment for me, before going on to represent the country at numerous World Cups and the World Championships in 2003. Competing in the senior competitions was very similar to the youth internationals. However, instead of being one of the best in the competitions, I was now having to face the challenge of working my way back up the ranks to the top again, and I had my sights set high. Since reaching my life goal of making the senior team, I had now decided my next aim was to compete at the most prestigious competition in the majority of sports, the Olympic Games. I absolutely loved being a fully fledged member of the GB team. I was living the life of a full time athlete, something I had

always wanted. However, being a regular senior international trampolinist brought with it a major commitment. As well as training nearly every day, I was away virtually every weekend, either attending National squads or competitions. Sometimes, if there were two World Cups on consecutive weekends, we would fly out on the Thursday, compete over the weekend, return home on the Monday, before flying out again two days later to the second World Cup. As a team we spent a lot of time together, everyone became close, we were like each others family. We understood what each other were going through, the pressure of competitions, being away from your friends and family. Although we competed against each other, the

ladies team bonded, and we became very good friends.

While at university it was easy to lead that lifestyle. I wish it could have carried on forever, but unfortunately I received no financial support and after leaving university, I had a decision to make. If I wanted to carry on training, which I definitely wanted to do, I needed to earn some money. My trampoline coach suggested I move in with her and earned money cleaning her house, which would allow me to train full time. I seriously considered it, but I was twenty one, had a boyfriend at home, and although I wanted to be a trampolinist and fulfill my dream of competing at the Olympics, I still had other goals I wanted to achieve in my life. Was it possible to achieve both? My dad questioned me, "what are you going to do when you stop trampolining? Unfortunately you can't trampoline forever", and he was right. I always knew at some point my sporting career would end and I had to have something I could fall back on when it did.

It wasn't an easy decision, but I moved home and looked for a job, not only so I had a career when I stopped trampolining, but so I could afford to continue training. Trying to keep up my training, and work full time was not going to be easy, but I had made that decision, so it was up to me to make it work. I also decided to continue training at my club near university. They had given me so much, and I believed the training I was receiving there was superior to any I would receive elsewhere. Back home it wasn't long before I found a job. I had specifically been looking for work which was not office hours. Ideally I needed shift work so I could have more days off to train. I found a job working in a fitness gym, which involved working from mid afternoon, "brilliant that gives me enough time to train in the morning then go straight to work" I told my boyfriend. So that's what I did. However, it was not as easy as I originally thought. Trying to train and compete as a full time athlete, as well as work full time, and be a daughter,granddaughter, sister, auntie, girlfriend and friend, just doesn't work. There are not enough hours in the day. I still enjoyed my training and really wanted to make it as an Olympic athlete, I just wished I didn't have to work to fund that dream! A

typical day involved, leaving for training at nine in the morning, driving one and a half hours there, training for two hours, then driving straight to work and working till ten thirty. I didn't have much time to myself. I was lucky I had an understanding
family and boyfriend. My boyfriend had been an international athlete in Martial Arts. Although he was now retired, he had been through the same challenges I faced, so fully understood the commitment needed to compete at the highest level.

Training and working so hard began taking its toll on my health. I refused to miss any training sessions, even if I wasn't feeling well, I still went and did as much as I could. I wanted to know I had done everything possible to remain on the GB team
and reach my ultimate goal. This meant not missing any training unless there was a good reason for it. I didn't realise the strain I was putting upon my body. I desperately wanted to make things work, and didn't want my trampolining to suffer
because I was working. The approaching season, 2004 was an important one, starting with the Olympic trials in which I was eager to do well. However, I was about to discover just how tired I was. It was the end of January and I was training hard, preparing for the first trial.
"Okay ready for one more vol?" my coach asked.
I thought for a second, I was shattered, but my routines had gone well and I did have a trial coming up,
"yeah okay, one more", I answered.
I began jumping, keen to complete one more routine, before making the trip home. My coach held the push in mat on the side of the trampoline, I could hear the sound of the trampoline springing up to its resting position as it propelled my tired body back into the air. I pushed down hard one final time on the trampoline bed, before raising my arms up, pushing my feet back and taking off for my first skill. A split second later in the middle of my move, I became disorientated seeing the bright lights of the ceiling. I realised I had lost where I was. As I tried to correct myself, I felt helpless as I fell towards the trampoline. I managed to get my feet

underneath me, but hit the
trampoline earlier than I expected, unable to prepare properly for landing. I felt a severe pain in my right ankle, realising immediately I had broken my leg. I was gutted. My first thoughts were to the trial,
"I'm sure it's just a sprain, I'll be okay. It can't be broken, I've got competitions coming up", I said, holding back the tears.

The doctors at the hospital confirmed my worst fears, my leg was broken, and it needed to be operated on. The doctors also discovered I had glandular fever. They couldn't believe I didn't know and had still been able to train and work while having it. I spent the next eight weeks in plaster, unable to do very much. The forced rest allowed my body time to recover from the glandular fever, as well as giving my bones time to heal. I had never been injured or gone this long without getting on a trampoline before, and after the initial few weeks, I was soon bored and
restless. Having such a busy, active life meant I was not used to having a lot of time on my hands. I was frustrated I had all this time yet I couldn't train. The weeks passed slowly and by the time I was out of plaster and given the all clear to jump it was the beginning of June. Once again, I was disappointed. I was now back jumping, but the qualifying competitions for that years National finals had finished, meaning I would not be eligible to compete in July. It would have been my tenth Nationals. Seeing how upset I was my coach approached the trampolining technical committee requesting special permission to allow me to jump, based on my status as a senior international. They had never given anyone a 'bye' to compete at this event before, but there is always a first, and I was given permission to jump. I was so pleased, I only had four weeks to get ready meaning I would compete a reduced difficulty routine, but it didn't matter. I just wanted to get back to competing again. I had not only missed training, but also the feeling of nerves and excitement that fill your body as you get ready to compete. There was nothing else that compared to the rush of adrenaline and feeling of satisfaction and pride I got when

I jumped well in front of judges and a big audience. It was eight months since I had last competed and I was excited that soon I would be able to experience those feelings I had missed so much.

CHAPTER 7: WELCOME TO THE REAL WORLD.

After returning from my injury, I decided something had to change. I could not continue working and training five days a week, it was too much. The dream of going to the Olympic Games was still alive so reducing my training was not an

option. It was my work that needed to change. My boyfriend suggested joining the ambulance service. He was a fireman and due to the long shifts worked, was given four clear days off a week, and the ambulance service was the same. I had never

considered joining the emergency services before, but the time off it gave you seemed ideal to enable me to meet my training requirements. So, later that year I did exactly that, became an ambulance technician. Working for the ambulance service was challenging, and at times emotional, but most importantly it was extremely rewarding. For the first time I had found something which gave me similar feelings to those I got when I trampolined well. The adrenaline rush I felt at competitions was similar to the one I received when faced with a crisis situation at work. Similarly, knowing I made a difference to someone's life, either by physically saving their life, or by simply helping an elderly person up after falling to the floor, gave me a feeling of immense satisfaction and pride. Had I possibly

found something that could replace trampolining when the time came for me to retire? "I think I probably have", I thought.

There was no denying the shifts were tiring and the nights long and at no point would I say it was easy, however it worked for me. I had a good income which I used to fund my training, travel and competitions, and I had reasonable amount of time off to train.

Ideally I would have liked more time, but I made the most of what I had. The 2005 season came and went, I jumped well, but had still not caught up from the time I had taken off with my leg. I made reserve for the World Championships team that year. I was not very happy, but I understood my injury had set me back. Fate would have it that I competed in the Worlds that year anyway, one of the team became injured, and as reserve it fell upon me to take her place. Again I completed my routines, but had not prepared adequately as I had spent my training preparing for the following season, I had not expected my services to be called upon! At around the same time, I became part of the World Class Development squad. Being a part of this programme meant I received a small
amount of funding. It also gave me access to some great services such as, a specialised strength and conditioning coach, a sports psychologist and a performance lifestyle advisor. It was a privilege being on the programme and regular meetings with the GB coaches to monitor my progress were also a part of the scheme. I remember one particular meeting with them. They asked me to rate myself on certain qualities, I'm unable to recall them all, but one was commitment. How committed did I think I was to achieving my dream goal of the Olympic Games? That was an easy one, I am 100% committed, I gave myself five out of five. When the meeting arrived, the coaches had also rated us on these qualities. The coaches gathered together, the head coach looked up making eye contact, I
smiled back waiting for him to speak.
"We have rated you four for commitment",
"Four?" I repeated, I was mortified. "Why a four?", I questioned.
They explained, because I was working full time I could not be 100% committed to trampolining. I couldn't believe it. So, because I have a job, specifically chosen because it gives me time and money to train, because I have never missed a competition or a squad, and because I use all my holiday allowance from work, to trampoline, I'm not committed? I was not happy, I felt insulted and let down by them. I had given everything to the sport and

to be told I was not as committed as others on the team, purely judged on the fact I had a job, was a real kick in the teeth. Sandra was in disbelief too, she had seen what I had sacrificed and together we were determined to prove them wrong. I would train harder, perform better and show them having a career, something to fall back on when I could not trampoline anymore, was not a hindrance. Surely the drive and motivation I displayed to hold down a full time job, and train were assets elite athletes should all have?

The following year, 2006, I again only achieved reserve place for the European Championships. I had taken a risk of putting a new, difficult move, called a triff, into my voluntary routine. The consequence of that was while I was establishing
the triff, some of my routines had not been up to the standard they normally were. I had still been selected to jump at some World Cups, but I was now looking at the bigger picture. A triff is a very complicated move. It involves doing three forward somersaults, with a half twist in the third. Only four women in GB had ever competed it before, but to make an impression and be competitive on the World stage it was a move I needed to accomplish. I had decided to use 2006 to establish my triff in competition, so in 2007, it would be perfected, ready for the Olympic trials in 2008. In trampolining only one man and one woman from each country compete in the Olympics, to be selected I would have to be ranked number one in the country. Ultimately I was preparing for 2012, to compete in front of a home crowd at the London Olympics, that would be amazing. Therefore, my plan was to earn the reserve position for Beijing, giving me the opportunity to experience the Olympic atmosphere, without the pressure of having to compete, all in preparation for London, 2012.

CHAPTER 8: DISASTER.

Saturday 24th February, 2007, started the same as any other Saturday. My now fiance, Steven was at work, I was on a day off, getting ready to make the familiar drive to training. My training at the start of the week had not gone very well, I had a terrible cold. I was still not feeling 100%, but the competition season started the following week and I needed to get some quality training in before then. Thankfully the drive was uneventful, there was nothing more frustrating than

getting stuck in traffic and being late. I remember singing along to Take That's, "Shine", on the radio, the weather was good and I was in high spirits ready for training. I walked into the sports hall, said hello to my friends, before jumping on

and getting myself warmed up. My friend Jane was training with me, we decided to help each other get our routines completed, so we could both go home and rest. After a couple of turns warming up, I soon got stuck in starting with my set. I

completed my set five times, but wasn't happy with how I was performing. This was normal for me, I suffered early with pre-competition nerves and they had definitely kicked in today. I was hard to please and very critical of myself, especially leading up to the start of the season. I decided to move on to my

voluntary which needed work, I couldn't spend all session trying to perfect my set.

After performing some triffs onto the mat, I was ready to attempt a routine. Although I was still feeling the effects of my cold, feeling tired and having trouble catching my breath, I told myself "only 3 routines to go then I can go home". I had

nothing planned for the following day, no training or work, I was looking forward to the well earned rest. While Jane was having her turn, I psyched myself up so I would be ready mentally and

physically to do my routine. I was listening to 8 mile,
by Eminem, it was the music I listened to before every competition, as soon as I heard it, it initiated feelings in me that helped me to focus. I chalked my hands and mounted the trampoline, leaving the usual two white hand prints on the side of the frame. Sandra was ready with the push in mat, which looked like the size of a postage stamp at my full height, but it gave me confidence having it there. I took a deep breath, shook my legs and started jumping. As I gained height, I could see the special needs group on the trampoline in front of me, their faces beaming in delight as they were gently bounced on the trampoline. I was aware of a fellow club mate on the bed next to me, waiting patiently for me to start. Once I reached a suitable height, made sure my jumps were powerful and well controlled, I told myself, "be strong", as I took off for my triff. A split second later my life would be changed forever.

After taking off for my triff, for some reason, I don't know why, I missed the exit point and stayed in the tucked shape rotating an extra half a somersault. This meant from a height of about 30 foot, I rotated three and a half times, landing on the back of my head with all my body weight on top of me. As I landed it was as if someone had pressed the slow motion button on the television. I heard a loud crack as I hit the trampoline, before being propelled back up into the air, with no control over my body, coming to rest on my back on the push in mat. I knew immediately what I had done.

Being a trained ambulance technician I recognised the classic signs. I had no movement or feeling from the chest down. I had pins and needles, and I could see my belly rising up and down as I tried to breathe. While Sandra arranged an ambulance and called my parents, I remained calm, keeping absolutely still. I asked for my phone and called Steven. He cheerily answered the phone and I told him,
"I've had an accident, its serious, I've broken my neck and para-

lysed myself",
before he could say anything, I continued,
"you're not going to leave me are you?",
I asked. While he absorbed the news I had just broken to him, I didn't get upset, I didn't cry, I simply explained,
"I'm waiting for the ambulance, can you meet me at
the hospital".
As I lay on the mat unable to move, I realised everything as I knew it would now be different. My mind wandered, I would probably never be able to get on a trampoline again, never drive an ambulance again, possibly never even walk again. It was too much to take in, but now wasn't the time to start dwelling on what may or may not be. There was nothing I could do to change what had happened. I had to be strong and concentrate on staying still. At that point my primary concern
was how the ambulance crew were going to get me off the trampoline without it moving, understanding the slightest movement could have further catastrophic consequences. I was worried about the thought of my life literally being in
someone else's hands. Eventually the ambulance crew arrived and very carefully and safely remove my helpless body from the trampoline. On the way to the hospital I managed to move my left foot inwards about a centimeter. It wasn't much and I had no other feeling or movement, but it was something. It was enough to give me hope and at that moment, when I had nothing else, hope was all I needed.

CHAPTER 9: A LIVING NIGHTMARE.

The next few days and weeks passed as a blur. My fiance, parents and sister met me at the hospital, where the nightmare I was in became reality. I had broken my neck and damaged my spinal cord and was lucky to be alive. I needed an operation
to stabilise the bones in my neck, so I was transferred to the specialist neurology unit at St. Georges hospital in London. I was initially on the high dependency unit waiting for an operation in a few days time. However, my breathing rapidly
deteriorated and I was admitted to the intensive care unit (ICU). I made no improvement so the doctors decided to intubate me, allowing a ventilator to take over my breathing until I was operated on. I said goodbye to my family, knowing I would be asleep for a few days. This would also be the last time I would be able to physically speak to them for a while. I was having a tracheostomy fitted to help with my breathing after the operation, which meant I would not be able to eat, drink
or speak until it was taken back out, and no one knew exactly when that would be.

The next thing I remember is being on the ICU a week after my operation. I was told it was successful, but nothing more. I had enormous gratitude to the surgeon who operated on me, he was like I was in my sport, at the very top of his game, a
very talented man. He had been able to maneuver within the intricate cavity of my neck, missing my trachea, vocal chords and other vital structures. A new disc between C6 and C7 had been created from bone taken from my right hip, replacing
the one I had shattered upon landing awkwardly on the trampo-

line. My vertebrae were then fused from the fifth, to the seventh with titanium plating, to strengthen my neck. I still had no movement, but insisted to everyone I would attend the

National finals in July as a spectator, and that despite what I was told, I would be walking in. My family never disagreed with me, never told me what the neurosurgeon told them. In fact I would not find out until three months later that they had been told, I would forever be in a wheelchair as I would never walk again. During these initial weeks of my injury I didn't have a chance to think about how my life would be. All my time and energy were focused on simply getting through each day, and a daily challenge was just trying to communicate with people. The tracheostomy tube prevented me speaking, leaving me to rely on the lip reading abilities of my visitors, which at times was not very good. I found it difficult to hide my frustration, often losing patience and refusing to try and communicate at all. As I lay there one afternoon, I recognised a figure walking through the ward towards my bed. As they approached I immediately recognised their face,

"What have you been up to young lady?".

It was Nigel. He had made the long drive from his home to come and see me as soon as he heard what had happened. I was surprised and honored. Even though I left him under a black cloud, he was my first trampoline coach, we had been through a lot together and still had mutual respect for one another. Seeing him lifted my spirits,

"You will be in trouble if you give up on me Nat",

I smiled, we both knew giving up was something I didn't do.

When I was well enough, I was transferred back to the ICU in the original hospital, to wait for a bed in a specialist spinal injury rehabilitation centre. The hospital I was in was 70 miles from home, so Steven and my mum moved up to live close to

the hospital while I was there. They were with me every minute of every day and continued to be throughout my rehab. The nights were the worst, I dreaded the moment when mum and Steven had to leave me there all alone. ICU's are not the

quietest places, and it's very difficult to get any proper sleep. I lay in my hospital bed, completely flat, staring at the only view I had, the ceiling. I lost count of how many times I counted the ceiling tiles. During the night even the dimmed lights seemed to shine brightly, the whole room lit up, so white and sterile. As I lay there trying to sleep I could hear the continuous beep of the machines, the pumping of the ventilators, the general chatter of the doctors and nurses working in this depressing place. Even if I managed to drop off, I was woken every four hours to be turned, unable to do it myself, to prevent pressure sores, and to be given the numerous medication I was now on. For someone who never even took paracetamol for a headache, it was difficult to accept my body now needed all these drugs to keep it working. I don't think I would pass a drugs test now I joked, sadly realising that was something I would never have to go through again.

Eventually after I felt like I had settled in, I was on the move again. A bed had come free in the ICU at Stanmore, the specialist spinal rehabilitation centre. Sometimes people can wait months for a bed, but I had only been waiting seven days which was great as it meant I could get stuck into my rehabilitation sooner rather than later. After an uncomfortable, bumpy ambulance transfer I arrived at the Royal National Orthopaedic hospital in Stanmore. Steven and I were shocked when I was wheeled into, what Steven described as a tin hut. I couldn't believe they were going to leave me here. I felt as if I was lying in a scout hut. This couldn't be right, this couldn't be the legendary Stanmore! I was assured it was and after meeting the friendly staff, and being reunited with mum, dad and Steven, I soon became more comfortable. I didn't have any choice really, like it or not, this hospital was going to be my home for the next few months.

CHAPTER 10: MOVING FORWARD.

After a few days, my consultant decided to start weaning me off the ventilator. It was a gradual process that had to be done in stages to enable my lungs to function independently again. It was a day that couldn't have come soon enough. I hated being constantly attached to this whirring machine, which my body had become so dependent upon. As the consultant prepared to turn the ventilator off, I felt nervous. I had doubts and fears that maybe I did still need help to breathe. Although I wanted to be free of the machine, it was a moment of realisation that I no longer knew my body, or its limits. It was not the same body I had lived in for twenty four years, the one I had known so well, confident of what it could do. I hadn't yet learnt the capabilities of my new body. The moment came when for the first time in almost ten weeks I would try to take my first breath of air unaided. The whirring of the machine stopped, everything was quiet. Everyone waited anxiously, watching me, would I be able to cope without the help of a machine. I opened my mouth, and took my first independent breath of air. I was on my own, no machine there to rely on. It felt great, I needn't have doubted my bodies capabilities just yet. I felt the air rushing in through my nose and mouth, inflating my lungs like balloons, and then passing gently back out. It was a strange feeling, a feeling so natural to healthy individuals but a feeling, like so many others, that had been taken away from me ten weeks ago. Having it back was something I relished. After a few good deep breaths, I began to relax and instead of consciously thinking about breathing in and out, the process became automatic once more. I turned to look at

Steven and my parents, I smiled, I knew exactly what they were waiting excitedly for,

"Hello", I said simply.

With the ventilator no longer attached to my tracheostomy, I was able to speak,

"It's so good to hear your voice", Mum and Dad agreed,

"Oh no, put her back on the ventilator before she starts nagging me" Steven joked.

To actually be able to speak, rather than mouthing the words was amazing. It was frustrating when people did not understand what I was saying, I had felt trapped in my body. At last I could tell people exactly what I thought and what I wanted. Today was a big step forward and a huge relief for everyone. Slowly I was regaining some independence, becoming myself again. I was like a wall that had once stood so strong and independent, but with one blow had been demolished. Now block by block, I was being rebuilt, it might take some time I thought, but today the first blocks had been laid.

Gradually the time I spent breathing without the ventilator increased, and it wasn't long before I no longer needed the support of the machine. My consultant was shocked at how quickly I learned to breathe on my own again, attributing the speed in which I moved through the process, to the high level of fitness I had prior to my accident. My lungs were in good condition and recovered quicker than a non athlete's would have. Once off the ventilator and able to speak, it was time to focus on my next challenge, eating and drinking. Nothing had passed my lips since having the tracheostomy and when I was finally allowed a sip of water, words can't describe how it felt. I can only imagine it being similar to how someone stranded in the Sahara desert, severely dehydrated, must feel. Water is not normally a drink I would choose, it's tasteless and there are a million other things I would rather have. However, that day I would not have cared if water was all I was ever going to be allowed. After having no problems swallowing liquid, food was my next task and I quickly advanced from chocolate mousse to fully cooked meals. Every progression I made, also meant a tube was removed from my body. When I was able to breathe alone, I lost the restrictive ventilator tube, after proving I could eat and drink, the uncomfortable feeding tube, which went in through my nose and into my stomach, known as a nasogastric tube, was also removed. Slowly not only did I begin to feel a bit more like myself, I also began to look more like the person I knew ten weeks ago. However, I was still a million miles away from anything resembling 'Natalie, the international trampolinist', and I began to wonder whether I would ever be able to relate to that person again.

This feeling was made even stronger after I was allowed to get out of bed for the first time. I don't know what I was expecting, but all the excitement and confidence I acquired from gaining some of my independence back, were knocked down, as the realisation of how little control I really had over my body hit me. Just to get out of bed took the help of four people and a machine called a hoist, which physically lifted me out of bed. I was helpless, like a baby. A big sling was placed under my body and attached to the hoist, reminding me of a small crane. The nurses maneuvered the hoist, with me hanging from it in the sling, lifting me from the bed and lowering me into a waiting wheelchair. I hated it, every minute of it. I wasn't strong enough to help them. If I wanted to move, the nurse had to do it for me, if I had an itch, someone had to scratch it for me. My feet were placed on the foot rests of the chair, a pillow under my arms. It had taken twenty minutes to get me into the chair, and I was only allowed to sit in it for fifteen minutes at a time. All that effort for fifteen minutes. I wondered if it was worth it. My family came in, seeing me out of bed for the first time since my accident. They were pleased, excited and cheerful, I was fed up, tired and depressed. The change of position, from lying to sitting, made me feel nauseous, and I couldn't speak, feeling as if I wasn't able to breathe properly. All I wanted to do was get back into the safety of my bed. How was I suppose to lead a 'normal' life if I could only sit up for fifteen minutes a time.

I didn't believe it would get easier, and struggled to understand how people in wheelchairs coped, there was no way they had ever felt like this, I thought. I felt very lonely and down. The extent of the irreversible damage I had caused my body

hit me. I just wanted this whole thing to be over. I wanted to go back to my old life, I didn't want to live this new life, I hated it and hated my new, useless body.

CHAPTER 11: NEW CHALLENGES.

My time on the ICU came to an end when I was deemed well enough to be moved to the rehabilitation ward. There was no ambulance required for the transfer this time, instead I was pushed on my bed up the steep hill of a corridor, around the corner to the spinal injury unit (SIU). Although I remained in the same hospital, once again I had to get used to the new staff, patients and rules on the ward. It was comforting knowing this was the final stage of my journey. The next transfer would be home, a place I was missing deeply, and had not returned to since breaking my neck. The rehabilitation ward was different to other hospital wards, I was encouraged to do things myself, to try and regain my independence. Being on the SIU also meant meeting other people who were experiencing similar things as I. I was sad and depressed as I realised nearly every patient there was wheeling themselves around in wheelchairs. There was not one patient who was able to walk. Despite what I saw, and knowing how weak my body was, I was still convinced I would walk out of there. I recalled the promise I made myself in ICU, I would walk into this years National finals. I refused to believe I would be confined to a wheelchair and would not let anybody tell me otherwise.

Part of rehabilitation involved daily physiotherapy and occupational therapy, which meant being allowed off the ward and into the gym. I was eager to start my physiotherapy and begin working my body again. When I was moved to the SIU, I had regained considerable movement in my left leg, and a little in my right. It wasn't much but I remember the day I first moved my right leg. I was lying in bed waiting for my morning medication. I looked at my right leg, willing it to move, concentrating hard on bending my knee. That's when it happened! My right knee bent upwards. It wasn't much, but I saw and felt a definite bend. I didn't tell anyone, I waited then tried again. I had previously moved my right leg in ICU but couldn't do it again, so I was told it was a spasm and not to raise my hopes. This time was different. When I tried the second time, my knee bent again. The adrenaline began rushing around my body. My heart rate increased and the butterflies I used to feel in my stomach when I competed reappeared. I just wanted to show somebody. As soon as my physiotherapists came in, I said calmly,

"I have something to show you".

I gathered all my strength and concentration and I did it, I bent my leg. They shared my excitement, smiling and congratulating me, it was a great feeling. It may only have been a small movement but the muscle was firing. Somehow the message was getting through my damaged spinal cord, from my brain, into my leg. It was a massive breakthrough.

I throughly enjoyed my time in the physiotherapy and occupational therapy gym. It was a welcoming change to lying in bed, staring at the same four walls. The gym also felt more like home. Most of my life had been spent in a gym environment, and it felt natural to be back in a similar environment. I approached my therapy sessions the only way I knew how, adopting the same mentality I used in my training. I set myself daily and weekly goals, even keeping a training diary, recording my exercises and monitoring my progress. However, this time my ultimate goal was not to compete at the Olympic Games, but was just as challenging, to learn how to walk again. In order to achieve my goal I worked hard in every single physiotherapy session, never missing an opportunity to get in the gym and regularly asking for extra physiotherapy. I was surprised when my physiotherapists explained, they liked working with me as I put in a lot of effort. I couldn't understand the attitude of my fellow patients, or 'inmates' as we called ourselves, all feeling like prisoners, trapped by our bodies and restricted to the boundaries of the hospital, but all desperately wanting to be allowed home. They would regularly miss their rehabilitation appointments, preferring to sleep or watch television. How could they expect to improve and get out of hospital if they didn't put the work in? Any exercises I was taught, I would do over and over, until I physically couldn't do anymore. I was so determined to get stronger. When I first got back on my feet, walking wobbly with crutches and the physiotherapists help, they banned me from using the crutches, taking them off me for the weekend. They had learnt quickly! Over the weekends, when there was nothing to do, Steven and I would sneakily push the boundaries, testing what I could and couldn't do. They would often return to work on Monday preparing themselves for what I had been up to. I think they secretly looked forward to listening to Steven and I telling them about our weekend adventures of how I tried to stand, to walk, or do wheelies in my chair!

I remember the first time I was allowed out of the confines of the ward. It was only for a few hours but I decided it was enough time for Steven to drive me to my trampoline club, back to where I had my accident. The nurses were shocked I
wanted to return there, even Steven was skeptical, but it was something I wanted to do, something I needed to do. I wanted to feel like me again, not just a hospital patient. As I still wasn't allowed home, it made perfect sense to me to return to the
closest thing I had to it, my trampoline club. I went in my wheelchair and as I got closer to the sports hall, I immediately recognised the sound of the trampolines, and the familiar smell of the gym, the chalk and the rubber mats. It was great being back seeing everyone training hard. However, it also made me realise, although my life had come to a halt, everyone else's hadn't. Life outside Stanmore carried on normally without me, nothing stopped because I was in hospital. After a few
minutes of watching people jump, I couldn't resist any longer, for

some reason I just desperately wanted to be on the trampoline. "I might not be able to jump on my feet, but I could still bounce on my bottom", I thought.

Steven reluctantly agreed, he had learnt by now if I set my mind on wanting to do something I would do it, with or without his help. So he lifted me up onto the trampoline, and I shuffled on my bottom, to the red centre cross. It was fantastic to be back on, "This is where I belong", I thought to myself.

I managed to rock the trampoline bed up and down, bouncing in a seated position. I don't know what it is, but there is something about the feeling of bouncing up and down on the trampoline that I love, I have done since the very first time I ever got on a trampoline, and despite everything I still had the same feelings.

I was becoming stronger every day, learning how to become independent and look after myself again. My goals of walking out of the hospital and at the trampolining National finals, were looking like they would become a reality. I gradually and tentatively progressed from wheelchair to crutches, crutches to walking sticks and lastly from two sticks to one. I couldn't walk very far, I was really slow, and although my walking was obviously not normal, as long as I physically left that hospital using my legs as a mode of transport, I didn't mind. It was a strange feeling walking around the ward. I was the only patient who had recovered well enough to walk. The staff and fellow patients were genuinely pleased to see me up and about, but I felt an incredible guilt that I was doing something I knew every single person admitted onto the ward wanted to do. Eventually my discharge date drew closer and I was soon packing my things, ready to leave. It is amazing how much I had accumulated in what had been my home for the past four months. I was full of excitement at the thought of finally being allowed home for longer than a weekend. I was also full of apprehension. Going home meant leaving the security and safety of the hospital, I could no longer pop along the corridor and speak to a nurse if I encountered any difficulties. I had the support of my family, but other than that we were on our own. This was certainly not the end of my journey, it was only the end of stage one. I still had a long way to go.

CHAPTER 12: A DIFFERENT LIFE.

Being back at home bought mixed emotions. I enjoyed the simple things I had waited so long for. The freedom of being in my own home, in my own bed and eating home cooked food. There were no more rude awakenings as the doctors did their early morning ward rounds, and the nights returned to being how they should be, quiet and restful. However, the initial relief of being home soon passed and the reality of how much I couldn't do and would never do sunk in. I was hugely dependent upon Steven and my parents, needing help with things including cooking, cleaning, gardening and shopping. However, before long Steven and my parents had to return to work and the days sitting alone at home became long and boring. I had never spent so much time sitting around. My life had always been packed full, rarely having a minute to spare, there couldn't have been a greater contrast. The consequence of my accident meant as well as not being able to trampoline, due to the physically demanding nature of my job, I could also no
longer work. I had nothing. Everything I had worked so hard for in my sport, and career, had gone in an instant. I was very despondent, I felt useless. What good was I to anyone?

When July arrived I attended the Nationals, my first year as a spectator. It felt strange watching the competition from the stands. I was used to being on the floor being watched, not in the crowd doing the watching. It was nice seeing my friends,
but it was difficult watching, knowing I would never be able to perform even the most basic skill on a trampoline again. As I watched the performers preparing to compete, I knew how they

were feeling. It took me back to the year before when I
had been in their position, praying I would jump well, knowing I would be devastated if I didn't. I thought how I would give anything to be able to jump again, even if it meant finishing in last place. So much had changed in a year. At the end of the first day, I was asked down on to the floor in front of the spectators, competitors, coaches and officials, some of whom had known me since I was eleven years old. As I walked in everyone clapped, giving me a standing ovation. It was an emotional moment and I did my very best to hold back my tears, but it was comforting to know I had the best wishes and support of so many people.

Trampolining had been part of my life since I could remember, and made up a huge part of me. Without it I felt lost. What was I going to do to fill the big void left in my life? I had lost my sport, my job, and my body as I knew it. I couldn't simply replace trampolining with another sport, or my job with another job. My new body placed limitations upon me, reducing my options of what I could do. I had always been an active person, proud of how strong and fit I was. Having an office job was something I promised myself I would never do, the thought of it bored me, but now it seemed I didn't have much choice. I spent hours sat at home wondering what to do with my life. I had it all planned out and now I had been forced to retire five
years earlier than planned, as well as losing my job, leaving me with nothing to fall back on to. The days became the same, each one rolling into the next. My family encouraged me to think of alternative career plans but nothing appealed to me. I
had lost all motivation, believing I had nothing to offer anyone. After losing everything I had previously gained self-esteem from, my confidence was at rock bottom.

After a few months, I slowly gained strength and adapted to my new way of living. I realised although my body is not in full working order, my mind was. How was I ever going to build a new identity and feel good about myself by sitting in my house? I thought long and hard about the direction I could take my life in. My real passion remained in sport. It was what I knew, and who I was. I knew I still wanted sport to be a major part of my life. Being in a gym and training environment, surrounded by individuals passionate about their sport, was where I was most comfortable. My decision was finally made when I went with Steven to his martial arts training session. It was a cold night, and the gym windows had steamed up from the heat radiating off everyones bodies, as they physically pushed themselves to the limit. The smell of gym mats and sweat lingered in the air, but being there strangely gave me a feeling of confidence. I was relaxed and enjoyed watching these people work themselves hard, never giving up, striving to be the best. I could relate to them. Although a part of me wished I could join in and have that feeling of exhaustion, knowing I have worked my body hard, I had to accept I couldn't. I could still help athletes though. I decided to use my sport science degree and apply to do a Masters degree in sport psychology, which had always been an interest of mine throughout my trampolining career, especially since I experienced LMS. Through becoming a sport psychologist, I would be surrounded with like minded people, in environments I felt comfortable and confident in and importantly help people improve and achieve in their sport. I also wanted to give something back to the sport I loved and missed so much. After speaking with Sandra, she explained despite my physical disabilities, I could still coach. I wasn't sure coaching would fill the gap, but it would keep me involved in trampolining. I was excited, but nervous about getting involved again. Would I feel bitter, resentful, even angry that I had been forced to retire? Initially it was hard being so close to trampolines, knowing I couldn't get on but I didn't feel angry or bitter, just sad. Due to the severity of my injury, I was lucky to be able to walk. Although losing my sport left a massive gap in my life, I realised I could have lost a whole lot more. I started coaching once a week at my club. It involved a 140 mile drive, but it was important to remain part of my club and trampolining, and it gave me the opportunity to see my coaches and training friends I have had for so long. My performers were only at the start of their trampoline career but I enjoyed seeing them progress. I received a sense of personal achievement when I saw them learn something new or achieve something they were struggling with.

As well as coaching, I began a sport psychology degree. After eighteen months of concentrating solely on trying to walk, and adapting to life as a disabled person, starting my academic studies gave me a different focus. I had spent so long feeling lost, lonely, and unsure of who I was, no longer known as the international trampolinist, but as the girl who broke her neck. However, my studies gave me a renewed purpose in life and something to devote my time to. I began to reinvent myself as a sport psychologist and trampoline coach. There is no doubt trampolining will always be in my heart, and a part of me will always be a trampolinist. However, through my work as a coach, and especially as a sport psychologist, I believe I have finally found something to take the place of trampolining. I hope to help people gain similar things from sport as I did. Being a trampolinist enabled me to travel, meet new people, gain confidence, self-respect and pride. It taught me commitment, hard work, dedication and to never give up. Although it was through my sport I became disabled, it was the assets I learnt from sport which got me through the lowest point in my life. Without them I would have given up, accepting life in a wheelchair. However, I am now looking forward to my new future and the challenges it will bring, and there is one thing I am certain of. Despite everything, if I could go back to that Saturday, when I was five years old, gazing across the sports hall to the trampolines, would I still wander over and start trampolining? Yes, without a doubt. I would not change a thing.

Printed in Great Britain
by Amazon